TOWEL ORIGAMI

Alison Jenkins

**Andrews McMeel
Publishing**

Kansas City

The Little Book of Towel Origami
copyright © 2008 by The Ivy Press Limited.

For information, write Andrews McMeel
Publishing, LLC, an Andrews McMeel Universal
company, 1130 Walnut Street,
Kansas City, MO 64106.

08 09 10 11 12 CTP 10 9 8 7 6 5 4 3 2

ISBN-13: 978-0-7407-7702-8
ISBN-10: 0-7407-7702-5
Library of Congress Control Number:
2008920752
www.andrewsmcmeel.com

This book was conceived,
designed, and produced by

Ivy Press

210 High Street, Lewes,
East Sussex, BN7 2NS, UK.

Creative Director Peter Bridgewater
Publisher Jason Hook
Editorial Director Caroline Earle
Senior Project Editor James Thomas
Art Director Clare Harris
Designer Joanna Clinch
Photographer Simon Punter

These projects were originally published in
The Lost Art of Towel Origami
copyright © 2005 by The Ivy Press Limited.

Introduction 4
Symbols and Folds 6

(10) **Happy Birthday**
(18) **Love Heart**
(26) **Cutie Pooch**
(34) **Tropical Palm**
(42) **Ladybug, Ladybug!**
(50) **Kiss Me Lips**
(58) **Lotus Flower**
(66) **Swimming Swan**
(74) **Monkey Business**
(82) **Elephant Ahoy!**

Templates 90
Index and Acknowledgments 96

Introduction

TOWEL ORIGAMI is one of the more intriguing arts once practiced by our forebears. Its exact origins are unknown but they have been the subject of much speculation. What is important is that this unique and ancient craft has been rediscovered!

The success or failure of traditional origami relies on accuracy and the need for straight, crisp creases in your material—but let's face it, towels just don't respond in the same way as paper. This permits a certain amount of artistic license in this far less disciplined, much more lighthearted form of origami.

Towel origami leans heavily toward a range of "molding" techniques, combined with simple, basic folding methods. All the models featured in this book have been created using these same methods, so you should be able to replicate them easily. Rest assured that towel origami requires no special skills, equipment, or even patience. Results are achieved in minutes and it's fun to do! A serious sense of humor is all that's required.

Begin by mastering the basic techniques, then move on to the individual projects. Each model has been awarded a difficulty rating, and it is recommended that you begin with an "easy" project and tackle a "moderate" or "difficult" one when you feel more confident. Whether you choose to fold towels for your own enjoyment or for the entertainment of your family or house guests, take pleasure in your newfound folding skills. Bath time will never, ever be the same again!

Symbols
and Folds

Due to the soft, fluffy nature of bath towels, the typical crisp folds that are the result of traditional paper origami cannot be recreated exactly. However, most of the very basic traditional folding techniques are employed, alongside more unusual methods, to produce very interesting creations. There is a certain amount of "molding" involved and a fair smattering of slightly more forceful manipulation, too!

Basic Symbols

-------- Dotted lines represent a fold line: either a fold that is made and left creased, or one that is opened out flat again to indicate the center or a division of the towel's length or width.

This symbol means that you must turn the whole shape over, keeping all previous folds or shaping intact. If necessary, slip one hand under the shape and place the other hand on top, then quickly flip it over.

⟶ Arrows indicate the direction in which the fabric of the towel should be folded, rolled, tucked, or drawn out.

Basic Folds

All the shapes in this book begin with a towel laid on a flat surface like the floor or a bed. Follow the instructions carefully, and always begin exactly as instructed with the towel laid out horizontally or vertically, as this will affect the final shape of your creation.

The Projects

Happy Birthday

We've called this classic model a birthday cake, but it would be just as suitable as a wedding gift or a thoughtful housewarming token. Simple white towels are set off with striking red satin ribbons, but a similarly delightful effect can be achieved by using pastel or even chocolate-brown towels, with lace or tassel trimmings. If you give this towel arrangement as a gift, wrap it up in a large square of clear cellophane so the layers keep their shape.

easy

YOU WILL NEED

2 BATH SHEETS
2 BATH TOWELS
2 HAND TOWELS
RIBBON TRIM
1 FACECLOTH

TOP TIP

As an extra treat, why not decorate the top of each layer with a row of colorful foil-wrapped chocolates or candies? These won't last till bath time, I can assure you!

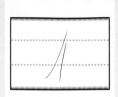

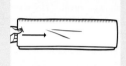

1 Lay one bath sheet out flat horizontally as shown and fold into thirds, folding the lower edge upward first so a fold, not an edge, lies across the top. If the towel is very wide, fold it into quarters.

2 Roll up the folded strip tightly from one end. Now fold the second bath sheet in the same way as the first.

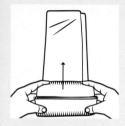

3 Pin the end of the second towel to the edge of the first and roll it tightly around the first roll.

4 Sit the resulting drum shape flat and secure the loose edges at the back using a few pins.

5 Make the second layer of the cake in the same way, but this time using the two bath towels. Secure the edges at the back and set on top of the bottom layer.

6 Make the third layer in the same way using the two hand towels, and arrange it on top of the first and second layers.

7 Wrap a length of colored satin ribbon around each layer of the "cake" and finish with pretty bows. You can use lace or other decorative trimmings or even cut-out paper bands, if you prefer.

8 Pick up a facecloth in the center and pinch it into points. Tuck the cloth into the top layer of the cake as a final decorative flourish.

Love
Heart

This one is an absolute must for all you true romantics out there—so simple to make and oh, so effective. Why not surprise your loved one on a special anniversary, a birthday, Valentine's Day, or indeed on a perfectly ordinary day! The sentiment will read loud and clear—a great big heart that says "I love you!" Aaaah!

easy

YOU WILL NEED

1 BATH TOWEL

TOP TIP

If your heart looks a bit flat, fold up two small matching facecloths and tuck them inside the heart shape to give it a plumper, more three-dimensional appearance.

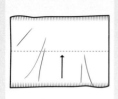

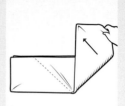

1 Lay the bath towel out flat horizontally, then fold in half lengthways. Press the fold flat, then fold in half widthways to indicate the center. Open the towel out flat again.

2 Place your left index finger at the base of the center crease, then bring the lower right-hand edge toward the center. Press the diagonal fold flat.

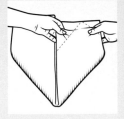

3 Fold the left-hand side likewise. Crease the towel about 4 in/10 cm down from the top along both short edges. This measurement may vary according to the size of the towel.

4 Tuck the short edges neatly behind the shape. Crease diagonally from the center of both short edges as shown.

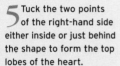

5 Tuck the two points of the right-hand side either inside or just behind the shape to form the top lobes of the heart.

6 Fold and shape the left-hand side of the heart shape in exactly the same way so it matches the right-hand side.

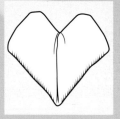

7 Make sure that all the corners are tucked in neatly and that the shape has a softly rounded edge.

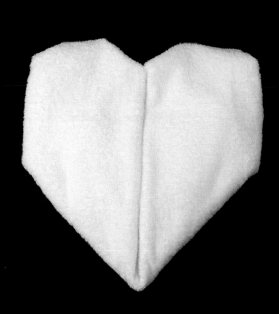

Cutie Pooch

I challenge even the most steadfast non-dog-lover not to adore this irresistible little pooch! Anyone, especially children, will love to see this friendly fellow greet them as they walk into their bedroom or bathroom. He's straightforward to make, and the quick addition of the felt features piles on the cheeky charm.

moderate

YOU WILL NEED

1 BATH SHEET
1 HAND TOWEL
BLACK, WHITE, AND RED FELT
1 SAFETY PIN

TOP TIP

Fido doesn't have to sit up all the time. Simply flatten the rolled-up leg shape so he appears to be lying down, then balance the head on the shape as before.

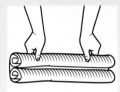

1 Lay the bath sheet out horizontally widthways, fold in half to indicate the center, then open out again. Now roll both the long edges toward the center.

2 Take the rolled shape and bend it to form the dog's body, making sure that the rolls are facing outward. Tuck one end of the shape under so it resembles the back legs in a sitting position.

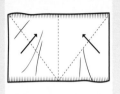
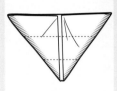

3 For the head, lay the hand towel out, fold in half widthways to indicate the center, then open out again. Now bring the two bottom corners to meet at the center of the top edge, then press the folds flat.

4 Fold the resulting triangle roughly into thirds horizontally as shown, press the folds flat to indicate the divisions, then open out the shape again.

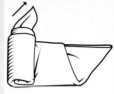

5 Fold the lower point up to meet the second division line, then fold the lower edge to meet the top edge as shown. Press the folded shape flat using the palm of your hand.

6 Take the point at each side and roll up tightly to meet at the center, then pull out the two points a little. Now secure the rolled shape using a safety pin.

7 Turn the shape over to the other side. Fold the points downward over the dog's face to form the ears. You can roll the edge that lies across the base of the points to release them a little more for shaping.

8 Balance the head on the body, apply a felt patch over one eye position, then add the felt eyes, nose, and tongue (see page 91 for templates) to give your pooch the cutest expression imaginable!

Tropical
Palm

Need a reminder of the beach when it's cold and snowy outside? You can re-create a taste of the tropics in your bathroom any time of year—Just use your bath towels! These amusing palm trees are so simple to make that in a short time you could create a whole desert island full of palms gently swaying in the breeze.

moderate

YOU WILL NEED

1 BATH TOWEL
5 FACECLOTHS
SAFETY PINS

TOP TIP

Use brown towels and green facecloths for an authentic look. You could also place colored round soaps or candy at the top of the trunk to look like coconuts. If something is worth doing, then it's worth overdoing!

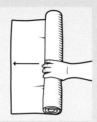

1 Lay the bath towel out flat horizontally and roll it up tightly and evenly across its width from the right-hand side to the left-hand side.

2 Grasp the roll firmly in one hand and find the corner of the towel inside the roll at the top. Pull the corner out of the roll to make the tapered tree trunk.

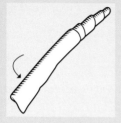

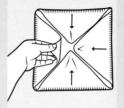

3 Next, tuck the lower ends of the trunk inside the lower rolled layers to make a thicker shape. Note: This shape will not stand up by itself and therefore must be displayed flat.

4 Now pick up a facecloth and bring all four corners together, making a pointed pyramid shape, as shown above.

5 Hold three corners in one hand, then pull the fourth downward to form a leafy palm shape. You can pin the folds of the palm leaf with a safety pin if necessary.

6 Do the same with the remaining facecloths to make four more palm leaf shapes. You can use more than five shapes if you fancy a really leafy palm tree.

7 Lay the tree on a flat surface and bend the shape slightly. Place the facecloth leaves at the top and arrange into a pleasing design.

Ladybug,
Ladybug!

Ladybug, ladybug, fly away home—but not until I've had a bath, if you don't mind! This brightly colored bug requires just a few basic folding techniques together with a little "molding" to achieve a nice plump final shape. The fluffy pipe-cleaner legs are not absolutely necessary, but they do make this creature look a bit more "bug-like," don't you think?

moderate

YOU WILL NEED

1 BATH TOWEL
3 FACECLOTHS
BLACK AND WHITE FELT
6 FLUFFY PIPE CLEANERS

TOP TIP

Red is the traditional color for a ladybug, but they do come in orange and yellow too, and some are even black with yellow or red spots. Just use your imagination.

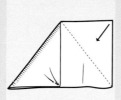

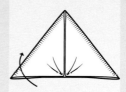

1 Lay the bath towel out flat horizontally, fold in half to indicate the center line, then open out again. Bring both top corners down to meet at the center.

2 Press the diagonal folds flat using the palm of your hand. Slip one hand under the shape and lay the other flat on the top. Now flip the shape over, inverting the triangle at the same time.

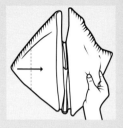

3 Fold the top two corners downward to meet at the center, and tuck the lower point inside the shape. Press all the folds flat.

4 Tuck the corners on both sides inside the body shape. This makes a more rounded silhouette. Fold up the two facecloths into quarters and tuck inside the wings to give the ladybug a plump body.

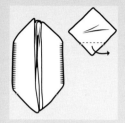

5 Take the third facecloth, tuck the lower point underneath, and press the fold flat using the palm of your hand.

6 Place the facecloth onto the top part of the ladybug shape, then tuck the three remaining points behind to form the head.

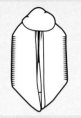

7 Now mold and shape the edges of the ladybug to make a smooth and softly rounded silhouette.

8 Add black felt circles for the spots and black and white circles for the eyes (see *page 95* for templates). To make the legs, fold and twist each pipe cleaner around itself.

Kiss Me Lips

Move over, Mae West! Salvador Dali designed a sofa in the shape of luscious red lips so we've done the same—well, almost—using a luxurious bath towel. What a fantastic way to give someone you love a big kiss! We've used a standard-sized white bath towel, but you can make a really big kiss using a bright red bath sheet if you want to make a stunning statement!

moderate

YOU WILL NEED

1 BATH TOWEL

TOP TIP

If you're not a purist, you can make your lips any color you like, bright pink, orange, purple . . . whatever takes your fancy.

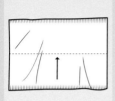

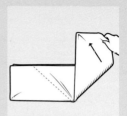

1 Lay the bath towel out flat horizontally, then fold in half by bringing the lower edge up to meet the upper edge. Press the fold flat using the palm of your hand.

2 Fold in half again widthways, press the fold flat to indicate the center line, then open out. Place your index finger at the base of the center line and bring the lower right-hand corner to lie along the center line.

3 Fold the left-hand side likewise, then slip your hand under the shape and place the other hand on top. Now flip the whole shape over to the other side, keeping the folds in place.

4 Fold and tuck the lower point underneath the shape to form the lower lip. Try a small fold first, then make it larger if necessary to achieve a pleasing shape.

5 Make a diagonal crease line from the center toward each of the top corners. Fold the right-hand shape along this line, then fold the left side likewise.

6 Now fold the top right-hand point downward to meet the center. This forms one half of the upper lip.

7 Now fold the top left-hand point to meet the center, then carefully arrange the bath towel so that no tapes or edges are visible.

8 For a special finishing touch, plump up the completed lips by tucking some chocolates inside the folds of the upper and lower lips.

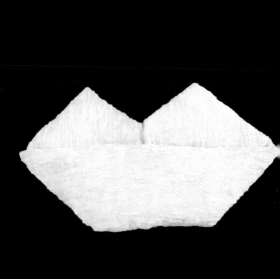

Lotus
Flower

This is a traditional, lovely design reminiscent of the folded linen napkins you may find adorning your table at a special restaurant. It is just as effective when translated into towel form, and very attractive if the colors you use coordinate with the decor in your guest's bedroom or bathroom.

difficult

YOU WILL NEED

3 BATH TOWELS
1 FACECLOTH
SAFETY PINS (OPTIONAL)

TOP TIP

If you wash and starch your towels first,
this model will stand up by itself. If not, lay it
flat or lean it against the pillows at the bed
head. You may even find room for it on a shelf
at the end of the bathtub.

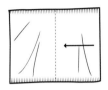

1 Lay one bath towel out flat horizontally, then fold in half widthways. Press the fold flat using the palm of your hand.

2 Fold the shape in half diagonally by bringing the lower right-hand corner up to meet the upper left-hand corner.

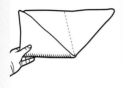
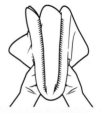

3 Place your index finger halfway along the diagonal edge and bring both the left- and the right-hand points toward the center. Press the shape firmly.

4 Keeping the shape flat, tuck the points at each side under the shape and pinch them together at the back.

5 Grasp the lower point in one hand, then peel the outer layers away from the central point to form a floral leafy shape.

6 Now peel the top layer of the central point outward and mold to make an even more pleasing and leafy shape.

7 Squeeze the shape so that it keeps together (you could use a safety pin to help with this), then use the remaining towels to make two identical shapes.

8 Place the three shapes together to form the lotus flower, then fold a small facecloth in the same way and place at the base to disguise the point where the three larger shapes meet.

Swimming
Swan

Seven swans a swimming? Well, maybe just one or two would be enough to make the point! This classic towel origami model demands to be created from the largest, fluffiest, and most luxurious of all the whitest towels you can find! This elegant bird works perfectly alone, or a pair can be used to great effect when arranged symmetrically.

difficult

YOU WILL NEED

1 BATH SHEET
SUNGLASSES
2 FACECLOTHS (OPTIONAL)
2 SAFETY PINS

TOP TIP

Why not make a few cygnets from facecloths
or small hand towels to complete the family
group? You could also place some attractive
fragrant soaps or bottles of bath product on the
swan's back for your guest to enjoy at bath time.

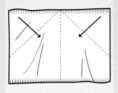

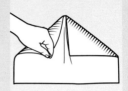

1 Lay out the bath sheet horizontally, then fold in half widthways to indicate the center and press the fold flat. Open up the towel again, then fold the top two corners down to meet at the center.

2 Press the diagonal folds flat using the palm of your hand. Now roll the towel tightly along the diagonal edge at both sides toward the center. As the towel is large it is best to do one side at a time.

3 When the first side is rolled up tightly, do the same on the other side so the shape is symmetrical. Make sure the first roll does not loosen as you complete the second.

4 Now slip one hand underneath the rolled-up shape and place the other hand on top. Quickly flip the shape over to the other side. This is the swan's body.

5 Place your hand on the swan's back and shape the rolled point to form the curved neck. You may have to use a little gentle force to make the neck stay in shape!

6 Locate the edge of the towel that lies across the rolled-up points at the back. Take the edge and roll it back on itself. This action will cause the points to splay outward.

7 Coax the points out a little more and arrange them to form the swan's wings. This will also help the stability of the shape. If you like, you can tuck a facecloth into each side to make the wings appear larger.

8 Add a pair of sunglasses to complete this elegant fowl. The weight of the sunglasses also helps to maintain the nicely curved shape of the neck. Use a couple of pins to keep the glasses in place.

Monkey
Business

This cheeky little guy can be arranged to sit on a bed or chair quite easily (although his head may need a little assistance from a safety pin). Use sunglasses to add character to his face or cut out some felt circles for eyes. The body holds together well allowing more scope for creative expression. You can hang him by one or both arms from a shower rail, using another safety pin to secure his arm so that he stays put!

difficult

YOU WILL NEED

1 BATH SHEET
1 HAND TOWEL
BLACK AND WHITE FELT
OR 2 CHOCOLATES
3 SAFETY PINS

TOP TIP

If you choose to use pins instead of safety
pins, make sure that they are large and have
colored-glass heads. This will ensure that they
do not get lost in the fluffy pile of the towel.

1 Lay the bath sheet out flat vertically, then fold in half widthways and press the fold flat to indicate the center, then open out flat again. Roll both the short edges tightly toward the center.

2 Grasp the rolled-up bath sheet in both hands and bend it in the middle. Make sure that the rolls do not loosen as you do so and that the rolls face outward.

3 Find the corner of the bath sheet inside each roll and pull each one out a little. Take two corners in each hand, then pull out firmly in the direction of the arrows. This can be a little difficult at first.

4 The rolls will tighten as you pull out the points, which in turn will twist to form the monkey's arms and legs. The area in the center can be manipulated to form the body.

5 For the head, lay the hand towel out flat, then fold in half widthways and press the fold flat. Now roll the towel diagonally from the top right- and bottom left-hand corners toward the center.

6 Hold the rolls in one hand, then roll the bottom point up toward the free points using the other hand. This will form a tight ball shape and the basis of the monkey's head.

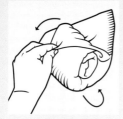

7 Turn the rolled shape over and peel the top layer of the point backward to cover the shape and to form the monkey's mouth. Tuck all the ends into the folds behind the head and secure using a safety pin.

8 Arrange the body so it can sit up or hang from the shower rail, then balance the head on top and secure with a safety pin. Attach felt eyes (see template on page 95), or small round chocolates using double-sided tape.

Elephant Ahoy!

What a surprise your guests will have to find an elephant on their bed! For an even bigger impact, try making a mini herd of jumbos, varying in size from a tiny one made using a facecloth and a small hand towel, to a real whopper made from a bath sheet and a large bath towel! This model works well in plain white towels, but for a really authentic look use gray ones. Or, for an amusing twist on the theme, use pink.

difficult

YOU WILL NEED

1 BATH TOWEL
1 HAND TOWEL
BLACK AND WHITE FELT
OR 2 CHOCOLATES
1 SAFETY PIN

TOP TIP

The rolled-up head and trunk shape
can sometimes unroll itself. Secure the shape
using a safety pin so that Jumbo won't lose
his head while in situ on your guest's bed or
in the bathroom!

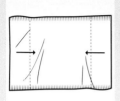

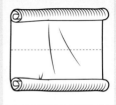

1 Lay the bath towel out flat horizontally, then fold along both short ends and press the folds flat. This will make the lower legs a little fatter so Jumbo can stand up by himself.

2 Now fold the towel in half lengthways. Press the fold flat to indicate the center and open out. Now roll the towel up tightly from both long edges so the rolls meet at the crease line in the center.

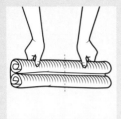

3 Grasp the rolled-up bath towel in both hands and bend it in the middle, keeping the rolled side facing outward. Try to make sure that the rolls do not loosen as you do this.

4 Stand the shape up and open out the rolls at the base of each "leg" if necessary so that Jumbo will stand sturdily on a flat surface. You have now completed the elephant's body.

5 For the head, lay the hand towel out flat, fold in half widthways, and press the fold flat to indicate the center. Open the towel out again, then bring both lower corners to meet the top edge at the center.

6 Roll both diagonal edges toward the center. It is best to do both sides at the same time, if possible. The point at the center will curl slightly, forming the trunk.

7 Turn the shape over and hold the trunk firmly in one hand, then pull down both upper points to form the ears. Open out the towel fabric a little to make a wider ear shape.

8 Place the head onto the body, then add a pair of eyes made from cut-out felt circles (see template on page 95), chocolates secured with double-sided tape, or sunglasses!

Templates

Accessorize your fabulous foldings with eyes, a nose, and other fun additions made from felt or construction paper. Use these life-size templates to create features for the models in this book.

1 Trace these shapes onto sheets of tracing paper, then cut out and pin to colored felt.

2 Cut out the shapes and apply to your model, fixing firmly in place using glass-headed pins or tabs of double-sided adhesive tape.

Cutie Pooch eyes

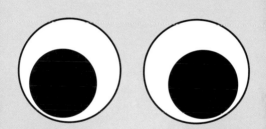

Cutie Pooch nose & eye patch

Cutie Pooch tongue

Ladybug spots

Eyes for all models

Index

B
birthday cake **see**
  happy birthday

C
cutie pooch 26-33
  templates 91-4

D
dog **see**
  cutie pooch

E
elephant **see**
  elephant ahoy!
elephant ahoy!
  82-9

F
folds
  basic 7

H
happy birthday
  10-17
heart
  see love heart

K
kiss me lips 50-7

L
ladybug, ladybug!
  42-9
  spots 48, 95
lips **see**
  kiss me lips
lotus flower 58-65
love heart 18-25

M
monkey business
  74-81

P
palm **see**
  tropical palm
paper origami 4

S
swan **see**
  swimming swan
swimming swan
  66-73

T
templates 90-5
eye patch 93
eyes 91, 95
  ladybug
  spots 95
nose 92
tongue 94
tropical palm
  34-41

Acknowledgments

The publishers are grateful to Christy
for supplying the towels used to make
the projects in this book.

www.christy-towels.com
Stockist number: 08457 585252